Contents

CW01496768

Foreword.

Get Your Head Out of the Sand.

The Science of Confidence – How to 'Man Up'

Powerful Strategies for Success.

Control Your Emotions and Stop Floundering!.

Think Fast, Think Smart, Think Before You Start.

About The Author.

Confidence Explained:

A Quick Guide to the Powerful Effects of the Confident and Open Mind

By C.K. Murray

Similar works by C.K. Murray:

Mindfulness Explained: The Mindful Solution to Stress, Depression, and Chronic Unhappiness

Emotional Intelligence Explained: How to Master Emotional Intelligence and Unlock Your True Ability

The Confidence Cure: Your Definitive Guide to Overcoming Low Self-Esteem, Learning Self-Love and Living Happily

Let Love Flourish: The Secret to Finding Your Kindred Heart

Body Language Explained: How to Master the Power of the Unconscious

Foreword

What if I told you that you could become more confident *today*? Would you believe me? Or would you put this book down, and think, *not more of this crap...*

But what if I told you that I *didn't* have the magic answer? That if you really, truly wanted to start feeling better *today*, you would have to put in some work... Would you keep reading?

Or would you think, *screw it?*

Truth be told, the answer is pretty easy. But it's also sometimes impossible.

Confidence is in all of us.

It's a part of us, a thought and feeling that floods our veins in moments of triumph, and abandons our bones when the world turns cold.

Every day, millions of people go about the drudgery of their lives, wishing for things to get better. Although they may spend their time wishing, they never act. They sit by and wonder *why, why; if only, if only*. No matter what, the confidence just *isn't* there...

Or is it?

In all the paths of life there are people, and voices, that may haunt us. These are voices that tell us we are incapable, powerless, ugly, stupid.

These are the voices that we blend with our own, losing track of who we are and where we're going.

But these voices will fade if we choose not to listen. Because everything, all of it, is a *choice*.

Oftentimes we hate ourselves for failure. Other times, we don't strive at all—we've already given up.

Sadly, happiness will always elude us if we can't accept our imperfections. Learning to be self-confident is about viewing life as a process. It is an experience that we can affect, we can change; it is not fixed, and it is not beyond our control.

If you think the 'river of life' is turning you over, maybe it's time to fight the rapids. We can't expect things to be offered to us. Sometimes our friends have easier lives than us. Sometimes, our lives take us to pinnacles we never imagined.

Life is about fight; it's about fighting for your dream, and your right, to shape your *own* reality, and make your *own* ripple in the pond. Believing in yourself starts with believing in your right to act.

What is your meaning—what makes your pulse jump?

Some of the most self-assured people in the world live without many of the things that we so often take for granted. In modern society, we are constantly surrounded by technologies that shape our world. We zip around on our smartphones, we check our friends on Twitter, we spend second after second, thought after breath, looking for the next thing, the next 'now'—because now's 'now' is not 'now' enough.

But why are we pressing so hard?

Maybe we've forgotten something. Something so simple and powerful, that its realization can instantly change our consciousness.

We've forgotten the simple power of belief.

Self-confidence is a powerful force. It is within grasp of every man and every woman who dares to examine. Any person willing to look deeper than distraction, and see that confidence is attainable, will benefit.

Why would you not be confident?

Those who possess high confidence are less likely to abuse drugs, commit crimes, fail school, practice unsafe sex, have unwanted pregnancies, crumble under stress, suffer eating disorders, engage in child and partner abuse, become financial dependents, grow depressed and attempt suicide.

So why again, would you *choose* not to be confident?

Confidence is as easy as it is difficult. In fact, it's so easy, that we don' have to do anything but think it. The problem is, we have to first *convince* ourselves that we can think it. This is the first step, and most of us will give up right away.

If we are to be more self-confident, we must learn to be open-minded. Being open-minded is a state of welcomed, receptive consciousness. When we are open-minded, we begin to see the world in a way that is utterly new.

Sustaining an open mind will make our lives less stressful and more uplifting. In fact, studies show that such a state of perception reduces progressive illness, and stabilizes various biometrics like breathing, blood pressure, heart rate, and brain waves. Living in a more accepting present allows our minds and bodies to work more synchronously with the natural world. It is, as they say, "the way nature intended."

People who are open-minded are happier, healthier, and more self-confident. They are more likely to acknowledge shortcomings and work to improve them. Because they make the most of the present moment, these people are less inclined to compulsive and impulsive behaviors. This leads to a noticeable reduction in mood disorders, anxiety and destructive behaviors.

Open-mindedness is about understanding that we can dictate, to a large extent, the power of life. We can learn to open up to those we care about. We can learn to self-heal, and to heal others.

We can learn to *no longer* hold back. To do what is intrinsically human; to love.

Open-mindedness is not some hippy mindset or politically affiliated manner of thinking. Open-mindedness isn't about having *no* opinion, or floating around in the ethers. Open-mindedness is about embracing the world.

It's about not shrinking back in fear when life has a little bite.

To fully comprehend how to become more self-confident, we must learn to undergo a variety of self-assessments. No, no, these typically don't require pen or pencil. What they *do* require is much more, and that's only part of it. You need to take a step back and realize, almost majestically, that life is there for you. You also need to start being honest, and maybe even stern with yourself.

You can't change without knowing what you want to change, and you won't know until you've thought over... well, until you've thought ov your thoughts.

So think about your thinking.

Where do your doubts come from? When do they rear their ugly head And why do you continue to feed them?

For me, self-confidence was simply gone. As much as I tried to tell myself of all the good things in my life, I just didn't care. My world existed in tunnel vision.

I never once looked into the sun.

I spent years hiding my alcohol and drug use from those I loved the most. I was afraid they would know and then they would try to help. I didn't want anybody to help—I didn't want anything.

All I wanted was to get away, and every chance I had, I ended up whe I had started. Trapped.

In my mind, I was not the one with the problem. It wasn't my probler because I wasn't the one doing it. It was society and friends and famil and all the *fucked up shit* in the world that was around me.

It wasn't me.

In my mind, I thought it was simple. If I wasn't the one in control, the

I wasn't the one responsible.

I lied to myself that this would make life manageable.

Yet, none of it made sense. Everything I did was a glaring insecurity. I spent so much damn time cultivating my bullshit that I lost track of who I was. I was one person this moment, and an alien the next. I was contradictory and confused, and I no longer knew if what I meant was what I thought or what I did was what I meant or what I thought I did meant anything at all or…

Most days my mind was gone, somewhere inside the sauce and the salt and the amp and the baby slits. But why was hiding?

Why couldn't I just be out with myself? Why hide behind a false face? Why was I so scared of a sober *me*?

I would never be confident, I thought. It just wasn't in my DNA. It wasn't in my neural chemistry, my brain or my thoughts. I was an addict; a loser; a complete dud.

But I was wrong.

Contrary to common belief, confidence is in all of us. It's not some gaudy and coveted chain that successful people wear on their thrones. It's not a mark of worldly beauty. It doesn't come with money, it doesn't come with attractiveness, it doesn't come with intelligence

Confidence comes from belief. Because without belief, the other stuff is just *stuff*.

When Charles Cooley devised the concept of the *looking-glass self* in

1902, he was imagining a reflective world. It was a reality that reflected our own insecurities and securities back onto us.

Along Cooley's line of thinking, every day is filled with moments of imagination. That is to say, every single day, and every interaction within that day, leads us to represent ourselves the way we *imagine* others to see us.

We create in our mind an image of how we appear to others. We imagine the way our words come off, how our emotions and feelings are interpreted. We think of the way our roles and actions are received by other people.

Maybe you say something and you think it's odd after the fact. So then what happens? Maybe you then feel nervous and think the person you are talking to will find you socially awkward. Or maybe you think the person will find you spunky and unique.

After we have imagined how we come off to others, we then begin to react to what we believe their judgment to be. If you do something and then a person says "Way to go," you can react a variety of ways. Perhaps you imagine that this person is being genuine and supportive. Or perhaps you imagine this person to be cynical and dry. As a result, we tend to act a certain way with a certain persona around certain people.

As interactions occur again and again, we begin to develop new layer after new layer. We interact and act based largely on the various symbols and meanings we attach to our encounters.

This forms the basis of Herbert Blumer's *Symbolic Interactionism.*

Basically, everything in our daily lives—people, places, and things—is ascribed a meaning based on our beliefs and our previous experiences. For one person, a church is a place of reflection and guidance. For another, a church represents evil; the evil preached by a drunk Catholic father.

This also ties into sociometer theory. In this theory, people construct their identities on the perceived evaluations and perceptions of others. There is no such thing as private reflection of self-worth; according to sociometrists, everything is connected with perceived judgments of others. Accordingly, "self-esteem" may in fact be "social-esteem."

Albert Bandura, the father of social learning, recognizes this distinction. Within his framework of social modeling, self-confidence is termed 'self-efficacy.' In essence, we develop senses of ourselves. With subsequent successes and failures, we learn what to expect and not to expect. We internalize an appraisal of our own abilities.

If we are in an environment saturated with positive words and visions, we are likely to challenge ourselves. If we are in an environment that is bleak, we are likely to sink.

Self-confidence comes from how we appraise our environment. It depends upon how we project ourselves onto others and how we imagine those others to project themselves onto us. It's a mostly unconscious process but we *can* change it.

But even the environment itself is a product of our perceptions. The worst job in the world cleaning sewage can be terrible to one person, yet for another person represent the first stepping stone in the sanitation business.

A person who works as a 'lowly' mailman may love his job because it creates a community feel, and because he loves driving down old neighborhoods, and he loves warm summer days with a cold Pepsi in the cup-holder and a clear road ahead. He may *honestly* think that nobody in the world has it better than him.

Another person might find the same circumstances intolerable. But that doesn't stop this second person from changing his or her thought process. From making the temporary job a tolerable if not slightly enjoyable task.

We just have to do a little work.

Still, making sense of this world can be extremely challenging. Things are never as they seem. People may not be who we think they are. Or perhaps people are everything we think and more.

Superstars adored the world over will sometimes crack. They may com undone in private, oftentimes to the shock of those who know them. Other times, our beloved stars will fade slowly, or blink out all at once, their ashes singed in the public eye.

Although confidence certainly exists in many highly successful people, not all of them are confident. And not all confident people are highly successful. Confidence can gain and wane throughout our lives, and it i important to realize this.

We are never too young or too old to make a change. Living in self-confidence is a factor in our daily lives. And with enough practice, it can become a part of us without so much as a *single* conscious thought.

Still, there is a fine line to be drawn, one that we all should note. Confidence does not equal arrogance. Arrogant people are not self-assured; they are insecure. They project their insecurities onto others. They present a false image; but deep down, they are scared shitless.

An arrogant person is not a confident person. Confidence does not attack.

Arrogant people feel the need to tell everybody how great they are because they depend on other people's opinions. Their inflated self-perceptions are fragile. These individuals are incapable of being truly confident, so they weave a new flesh, a new front, a deceptive persona—one that attacks others to preserve itself.

Arrogance is weak. Confidence is an emblem of strength.

There ain't a clean road that will lead you to perfection. You can't instantly erase your every fear and insecurity. However, you can change, day by day. Confidence is a pattern of thoughts and behaviors. If we can get our minds and bodies in a rhythm, feeling good and doing good become second-nature.

When we are confident, we make it a habit to think more positively and act more positively. That's not to say that things won't get rocky from time to time. After all, it is easy to come apart when the day is long and every little detail seems to be going wrong. You might feel like you're suffocating, like everything is closing in.

This is where we take a crucial step. By acknowledging that we will never be flawless.

A confident person will plan for success. A confident person will not be afraid to seek resources for help, and will value new relations as opportunities for growth. A confident person does not profess to have all figured out. A confident person may even admit that he or she knows very little.

And that's why a confident person can *bloom*.

People with low confidence may stop trying because they tell themselves, why try? When people make excuses, they stop trying. An once they've stopped trying, they feel trapped. Instead of working to free themselves and feel better, they remain trapped and feel worse.

Anybody can *exist*. Living is a whole other thing...

Confidence is visible. Confident people exude an air; an aura. They do not shrivel at the slightest thought of stress. They do not demean themselves for every little thing. Confident people tackle stress and ris to the occasion.

We are all capable of incredible things, but without the initial belief th we can do those things, how will we ever do them? If you don't think you can do something, are you likely to attempt it?

This is why confidence is invaluable. Without confidence, we will believe that we are broken. We will let every moment pass us by, because we are afraid of the possible negatives. People without confidence *expect* to fail. They see the world in black and white. In reality, there are a hundred shades of grey. And I'm not talking about erotic novel…

Expecting to fail and never acting is worse than actually failing. Think about it. At least when we fail we can grow. What good does sitting around do you?

At the end of the day, a confident person understands one thing. Through all our daily struggles with work, with peers and bosses, friends and family, life and death, lost dreams and crushed hopes—through everything, we *choose* to be confident.

Failure is always possible; but it never has to be *probable*.

Get Your Head Out of the Sand

If you believe in yourself, you are well on your way.

Now that you understand failure, and accept it as a possibility; now that you plan for success as not only a possibility, but a likelihood, you are ready to bloom.

But how do I remain self-confident?

Sometimes life is so unpredictable, we feel lost. There are days when tragedy strikes and days when everything simply flows. Although we may tell ourselves that we are confident and in control, the world has a way of knocking us down.

Losing a job or a loved one or a treasured ability can be devastating. Sudden, powerful events can change our lives forever. Some days the wind blows, the storm roars, the mind shudders, and all we can do is hold on for dear life.

Believing in ourselves is invaluable. When we tell ourselves that we are loved, worthy, and meaningful, we begin to realize that life really is what we make it.

Don't forget, confidence is a pattern of behaviors and thoughts. Sometimes, when cataclysm strikes, we want nothing more than to retreat. In rare cases, we shut down entirely. If you feel that life is testing you and you *just* don't have what it takes, maybe it's time to change your perspective.

Believing that we are powerless is a result of everything that has happened to us. But more than that, it is a *perception* of everything that has happened to us. If the same exact thing happens to two people, one person may break while another person grows stronger. Some of us may abuse drugs, some of us may jump into bad relationships, some of us may simply pull back from the world altogether.

It happens. People who were happy and loving transform, seemingly overnight. The strong become weak. The happy turn sad. Our *schemata*, the perceptual framework of our lives, change.

And we lose our confidence.

Not everybody has life in check. Some people may believe in themselves, but they only use that confidence for bad, ending in crime or heartbreak. Other people are only confident in very narrow areas, leaving them with few options for change.

No matter how you choose to structure your life, where you plan to go, you should make decisions that guide you there.

Even when things go haywire, we stay true to ourselves. We remain tied to our visions; our dreams. We act in accordance with our beliefs. If we're confident, we'll work toward those goals. We'll commit to acting as we know we can and *should*.

Confidence is about life.

It's about admiring what others have accomplished. It's about growing strong and powerful, thinking and doing and channeling our power without worrying about other people's opinions. Sure, we should acknowledge opposing opinions, but confidence doesn't *acquiesce* to those opinions.

Take the time to find out what you want from life, and act to get it. And don't, *don't*, let another person's failures tarnish your successes.

Confidence is about staring down your reflections, the many monsters of your past, and *smiling*. After all, your journey is yours and only *you* can choose who to let into your wondrous little world. You've certainly messed up, and you've certainly missed a step—but that's why you're here today.

You're here today because of the choices you've made. Now it's decision time. What choices will you make now? And where will they take you tomorrow?

Will you bloom or will you wither?

Being a confident person doesn't mean that you are the coolest kat on the block. It doesn't mean men and women adore you and it can't be quantified in terms of salary, hours worked, or number of sports cars owned. It's not about the size of your house or the value of your jewelry, or the number of fresh clothes and new shoes.

When you are confident, you don't need to brag. Confidence is not an investment in material possessions; it is not a preoccupation with *things*. Confident people can want *things* just like anybody else; they just don't *need* things.

A confident person will wear a suit or a dress. A confident people will wear this suit or dress because a confident person is comfortable in the suit or the dress. The suit or dress is not the source of this belief. The suit or dress is merely a marker. For an unconfident person, that same suit or dress is different.

For an unconfident person, the suit is pretentious and the dress is too showy. He or she doesn't feel right, doesn't deserve it. A confident person is confident no matter the suit or dress, no matter the skin.

A confident person is comfortable in the skin they're in.

When other opinions contrary to our own filter through our senses, we need to take the time to listen. This doesn't mean we change our own views, but at the very least, we think about what we've heard, how it relates, and how it fits with the person we want to be.

When we're true to ourselves, we evolve. We are refining and redefining our thoughts, emotions, and behaviors. This is the basis of what therapists call "Cognitive Behavioral Therapy." By examining our belief systems, and the thought processes behind them, we change our worlds.

Our power is in this commitment to ourselves. We are bent on becoming the best 'me' we can be.

When we are *not* focused on being the best 'me' we can be, we make a habit of thinking negatively. We blame others, or we blame ourselves- we blame, and we sulk, and we withdraw. We resign to inaction. And then we wait, for others to help us. For others to bring us what we *thin* we can't get ourselves.

When thinking of confidence, it is important to think of what researchers call 'the placebo effect.' Although many people will demean the term by saying, "it was just a placebo effect," most of thes same people have no idea what they're saying.

Just a placebo effect?

The placebo effect is amazing when we think about it. What this mear is that our mind is capable of making something real, simply by believing it's real. People are given pills and told that the pills will improve this or that. Even if there is nothing in the pill, many of these people end up experiencing some of the expected effects.

Simply because they *believed* it would happen.

The same thing happens when we *believe* that we can achieve our goa and survive our days. We look to a positive future with a positive mindset. And we recognize, almost magically, that the power is suddenly ours.

And this power is everywhere. According to Albert Bandura, the hum being is an amazing creature that creates *symbols* in order to make sense of life. We gain or lose power by the way we devise these symbols. Symbolizing happens on such a fundamental level that we often don't realize we are doing it.

Think about it.

Everything in our environment is given a meaning. A doctor's office symbolizes cleanliness and health. Or for another person, it might represent fear and needles. Ball parks may symbolize fun and drunkenness for one person and social anxiety for another. Smoking cigarettes may represent a temporary fix for one person and a debilitating addiction for another.

By symbolizing, we create guides for action, we solve problems, we plan thoughtfully, and we communicate through parameters of time and distance. Our power is gained by negotiating the crazy world around us. And negotiate we must…

Symbol creation begins from a young age.

When parents provide acceptance, children receive the building blocks for confidence. If one or both parents are overly critical, or if they hover over their children and protect them from every little perceived threat, children may never develop confidence. When parents guide children's progression toward self-reliance, children learn to deal with success and failure on their own terms. They learn to accept themselves or change what they don't like.

The bottom line is simple: we need symbols to make sense of our lives. We need them for self-direction and planning. We need them to set goals and challenge ourselves, to motivate and regulate how we behave.

Through symbols we can all be stronger than we think we are.

But what if that's not enough? What is the science behind confidence?

The Science of Confidence – How to 'Man Up'

For years I was convinced that if I couldn't control *everything*, there was no point to controlling *anything*. We're all just dust particles and matter. We'll fade and the world will go on and the sun will keep rising and the years will pass, and my existence will be forgotten.

And no psychologist with a fancy degree from a prestigious school was going to tell me otherwise.

And so I stayed as far away from control as I could. I pumped my body with whatever I could find to keep from thinking. If I couldn't control myself then I couldn't be responsible. If I was powerless, it wasn't me doing it. Some people filled their daily lives with religion to give themselves purpose.

I filled my days with toxins, to *remove* purpose. I was no longer in control. I stole and I lied and I manipulated, anything to get what I needed. And when anybody, *anybody*, made me face the reality of my actions, I denied.

But why did I act this way? Was it something in my brain—some abnormality? Why couldn't I believe that things mattered, that I mattered, that life was here for me to enjoy, and that being happy and confident would make that enjoyment all the sweeter?

What the *fuck* had crawled into my head?

What I failed to realize was that I *was* in control. *I* was the one making the choice to abuse alcohol and drugs. *I* was the one who picked up the bottle and opened the pill container and called up my 'buddy' to get more of whatever I wanted whenever I wanted it.

It took me a long time to realize it, but I could *choose* to be confident. And I could *choose* to stay committed to that lifestyle of confident, healthy choices. Or I could choose to rot away and leave this life behind.

And it all starts with the brain…

Now, I'm no neuroscientist by any stretch, but I *do* have a general understanding of the process. The brain is vastly complex, as you know, and theories on the brain are continuing to evolve, as you know. When it comes to that bundle of grey matter, it all starts with neurons. Neurons are cells that shoot chemical and electrical signals through your brain's wiring. Neurons form 'neural networks' and it is these networks that interconnect our brains and link to various regions responsible for various thoughts, feelings, and behaviors.

When neurons fire signals, they are essentially communicating. These messages are called "neurotransmitters," and they cross gaps called "synapses."

The gadgetry of the human mind is always in flux. One of the most important pieces of circuitry is called the reward pathway, and it is this 'pathway' that plays such an important role in behavior. Because the reward pathway connects to other parts of the brain, it is tightly bound to our five senses.

When we kiss a loved one, the senses let us know that what we are doing feels good, and the neurotransmitter dopamine is released. This important neurotransmitter gives us the feeling of pleasure that the brain remembers. As a result, memories of the pleasurable experience are gathered and the reward pathway reinforces the behavior.

The reward pathway even connects to the brain's motor center to strengthen the wiring for the necessary movements. This can range from the motions involved in massaging your significant other, to the movement involved in pleasurable activities like jogging or yoga.

Typically, when we lack confidence in ourselves, our reward pathway is not getting what it needs. As a result, our brains are under-stimulated and will often leave us with no choice but to seek a 'stimulating' activity.

In the unconfident mind, where negativity and pessimism preside, these activities are often maladaptive. Such as drugs.

The power of low self-esteem is strong. In fact, diminishing self-esteem is associated with increased activity in the bilateral anterior insula, a region believed responsible for reactions to rejection and distress. Some regions, related to the understanding of other people's minds, also play a role in lowered confidence.

Some studies have focused on another part of the brain, the posterior insula. This region is responsible for rewarding behaviors of positive social interaction and has been shown to 'excite' during measures of high self-esteem. This part of the brain also goes off when we are touched. Thus, researchers surmise that positive social feedback is a form of 'emotional touching.' A nice physical touch makes us feel good and confident, just like the nice 'touch' of a pleasant interaction.

Of course, all of this bonding and attaching begins very early in the human life. As naturally social creatures, we depend upon caretakers up until a certain age. Babies simply cannot survive without an older human being to give them what they need. Even at the tender age of 16-months, human security and confidence can be studied.

One such 2007 study assessed secure and insecure attachments between infants and mothers. Infants watched two videos, one of a mother walking up a stairwell and leaving a crying baby behind, and another of a mother walking up the stairwell and then coming back down to get the crying baby. Researchers found that insecurely attached babies showed surprise, and watched longer, when the mother actually came back. In fact, insecurely attached babies didn't even seem fazed by the video of the mother walking away and not returning. They *expected* rejection and abandonment, and were surprised to see a caring mother.

This lack of security represents not only a lack of confidence in others, but a lack of confidence in oneself. In adults, this leads to behaviors and attitudes that reflect a general sense of worthlessness. Like the insecure babies in the studies, similar adults will anxiously expect negative social reactions, will interpret negativity when there is none, will undermine otherwise healthy relationships, and become less engaged and have less success in academic arenas. In short, an adult with low self-confidence will come to expect rejection and conflict, because, well, they *deserve* it anyway...

Of course, it is also important to take into account the genders of participants in such studies. In general, gendered differences in self-confidence are now acknowledged. Women are believed to relate self-esteem more to social acceptance and bonding, whereas men attribute confidence more closely to some objective standard of success, like career trajectory or annual salary.

But it gets even more interesting. When examining the power of belief on self-confidence, race divisions play an important role. When Walton and Cohen (2007) created an experimental intervention targeting first-year African American college students, they weren't entirely sure what to expect. Nonetheless, they set out with the goal of boosting all confidence levels. Participants in the experimental group were told that doubts about their belonging were totally natural but would quickly subside. They viewed countless statistics, listened to speeches about upperclassmen, and were required to write essays exploring how perceptions of African American students could change for the better.

By contrast, those in the control group were given similar activities, but with a slight difference. Instead of being fed positive statistics and messages, these participants received information that did not reinforce any particular notions about black students, one way or the other.

In the end, the results were significant. Those in the experimental group were more resilient, took more challenges, showed no motivation changes on high-adversity days, contacted professors more often, studied more often, and received higher grades. More specifically, participants in the experimental group emailed professors 3 times as often as the control group, and control group participants showed substantial drops in motivation when adversity increased.

Yet another study *illuminating* the power of self-belief and self-confidence on real-world performance...

The power of self-confidence comes mostly from the appraisal of one's ability. When people believe that their abilities are largely fixed, they are less likely to work to change.

This idea has been researched more extensively in recent years, especially in the area of parent-child dynamics. What researchers find is quite interesting. Although many parents believe that positive reinforcement is *always* a good thing, experts are warning against this.

The devil is in the details. Parents with the best intentions will assure a child, "honey, you're plenty smart enough." Another parent might tell a kid that, "you're athletic, just like your father."

The problem with these types of comments is that they attribute fixedness to the positive quality. In fact, many gifted students who learn at a young age from their parents that they are "bright," end up underachieving. Just as a student will believe he or she is stupid and not work to change it, a student who believes he or she is smart will also not work hard to change it. As a result, when negative results like mistakes or poor grades or test results occur, both 'bright' and 'dim' students will be less confident, and less inclined to work for change.

The 'bright' student might internalize, "I'm smart, I just don't care," and the 'dim' student might think, "See, I knew I was dumb."

In 2007, Blackwell, Trzesniewski, and Dweck executed a "malleable-intelligence intervention" with students making the transition from elementary to junior high school. Both the experimental and control groups received a multi-session workshop designed to boost study habits, but the malleable-intelligence group was additionally told that the human brain is a muscle capable of forming new connections every time it is 'flexed.'

In the end, students in the control group showed no improvement in motivation or grades, whereas the malleable-group students exhibited significant gains in both areas, grades especially.

Of course, this opens up a whole new bag of issues—namely, what good are grades? A lot of school researchers lament that this practice has superseded *non*-graded, formative assessments of student learning. Many researchers believe that non-graded assessments provide feedback to students as they learn, help motivate them, and encourage them to be self-regulated learners.

Unfortunately, state-wide tests make these types of assessments hard to administer. While teachers may use their own student-level assessmen (tests, quizzes, homework, problem sets) to monitor learning, it is challenging to use performance on classroom measures to predict performance on external measures such as the statewide tests or nationally normed standardized tests like the SAT, ACT, GRE, etc.

Furthermore, invalid grades that understate the student's knowledge may prevent a student with ability from pursuing certain educational o career opportunities.

Speaking of career opportunities, self-confidence is an important prerequisite. Just as studies measure how students achieve based upon their self-beliefs, professionals also experience similar gains and losse depending upon their changing confidence levels.

Fostering self-esteem in the workplace is now a critical part of many business models. Farmers are taught that self-confidence is more important than innovative farming technology. Bankers are taught that strengthening client self-confidence will increase the bottom line; such clients are believed more likely to pay loans and provide good business. Management consultants, especially, preach the power of confidence in order for staff to meet company goals.

Confidence, confidence, confidence. Some people may throw their hands up and say it's a bunch of psycho-jargon, a bunch of mumbo-jumbo—but the studies don't lie.

Confidence makes a very real and measurable impact on both the personal and global level. Confidence sustains, and *enhances*, life.

But how confident are *you*?

Do you have any idea where you stand, compared to the 'norm'? Do you assume you're average, below average, well below average?

Dr. Rosenberg's Self-Esteem Scale is one of the most widely used scales in sociology and psychology today. Take a look, and see where you stand.

For items 1,2,4,6,7: Strongly Agree=3, Agree=2, Disagree=1, and Strongly Disagree=0. For items 3,5,8,9,10, noted by asterisks, Strongly Agree=0, Agree=1, Disagree=2, and Strongly Disagree=3. The higher the score, the more confident you likely are.

I feel that I'm a person of worth, at least on an equal plane with others.
I feel that I have a number of good qualities.
All in all, I am inclined to feel that I am a failure.**
I am able to do things as well as most other people.
I feel I do not have much to be proud of.**
I take a positive attitude toward myself.
On the whole, I am satisfied with myself.
I wish I could have more respect for myself.**
I certainly feel useless at times.**
At times I think I am no good at all.**

So now what?

Well, let's look at another scale for you...

Julian Rotter devised the notion of *locus of control* in the 1950s, a term that has spawned a variety of psychological and social research. Basically, the locus or location of our control runs on a continuum from internal to external. If it is external, we believe things outside ourselves control us. If it is internal, we believe that *we* control ourselves.

Having a more internal locus of control means that we hold ourselves accountable. We attribute successes and failures to our own doings. This can be a good and a bad thing. If we attribute failures to ourselves all the time, we may be ignoring powerful external factors.

We may be pressuring ourselves unrealistically to be perfect.

However, having a strong internal locus of control can also be beneficial. We will attribute most of our successes to our own doings, and subsequently increase our self-belief. By having the right combination of confidence, commitment, and control, we learn to appraise successes and failures as contributing to personal growth.

Failures do not debilitate us, and successes do not make us arrogant. Instead, we learn to exercise control wherever possible, while still acknowledging outside factors that can possibly affect us.

A person with confidence, commitment and control will transcend. Even if that transcending is not *entirely* under their control.

Steven Nowicki and Bonnie Strickland created a scale to in the 70s that measures the exact concept of *locus of control,* geared especially toward adults.

Test yourself and see where you stand. Answer simply yes or no:

1. Do you believe that most problems will solve themselves if you don't fool with them?

2. Do you believe that you can stop yourself from catching a cold?

3. Are some people just born lucky?

4. Most of the time, do you feel that getting good grades means a great deal to you?

5. Are you often blamed for things that just aren't your fault?

6. Do you believe that if somebody studies hard enough, he or she can pass any subject?

7. Do you feel that most of the time it doesn't pay to try hard because things never turn outright anyway?

8. Do you feel that if things start out well in the morning that it's going to be a great day, no

matter what you do?

9. Do you feel that most of the time parents listen to what their children have to say?

10. Do you believe that wishing can make good things happen?

11. When you get criticized, does it usually seem it's for no good reason at all?

12. Most of the time do you find it hard to change a friend's (min● opinion?

13. Do you think that cheering, more than luck, helps a team to win?

14. Do you feel that it is nearly impossible to change your parents' mind about anything?

15. Do you believe that your parents should allow you to make most of your own decisions?

16. Do you feel that when you do something wrong there's very little you can do to make it right?

17. Do you believe that most people are just born good at sports?

18. Are most of the other people your age and sex stronger than you are?

19. Do you feel that one of the best ways to handle most problems is just not to think about

them?

20. Do you feel that you have a lot of choice in deciding whom your friends are?

21. If you find a four leaf clover, do you believe that it might bring good luck?

22. Do you often feel that whether or not you do your homework has much to do with what kinds of grades you get?

23. Do you feel that when a person your age is angry with you,

there's little you can do to stop him or her?

24. Have you ever had a good luck charm?

25. Do you believe that whether or not people like you depends on how you act?

26. Will your parents usually help you if you ask them to?

27. Have you ever felt that when people were angry with you, it was usually for no reason at all?

28. Most of the time, do you feel that you can change what might happen tomorrow by what you do today?

29. Do you believe that when bad things are going to happen they just are going to happen no matter what you do to try to stop them?

30. Do you think that people can get their own way if they just keep trying?

31. Most of the time, do you find it useless to try to get your own way at home?

32. Do you feel that when good things happen, they happen because of hard work?

33. Do you feel that when somebody your age wants to be your enemy, there's little you can do to change matters?

34. Do you feel that it's easy to get friends to do what you want them to do?

35. Do you usually feel that you have little to say about what you get to eat at home?

36. Do you feel that when someone doesn't like you there's little you can do about it?

37. Do you usually feel that it is almost useless to try in school because most other students are just plain smarter than you are?

38. Are you the kind of person that believes that planning ahead makes things turn out better?

39. Most of the time, do you feel that you have little to say about what your family decides to do?

40. Do you think it's better to be smart than to be lucky?

Notice that when people have a very external locus of control, they assume that it doesn't really matter what they do. No matter what, life will fall into place according to *others'* wants and needs.

This is an important finding echoed in studies across the world. Adults with strong internal loci of control tend to also have low self-efficacy. Due to their fragile confidence levels, these adults will assume that they are largely incapable of changing their lives.

Those who underachieve in all walks of life tend to assume that things will continue the way they are.

In physics terms, objects in motion tend to stay in motion; objects at rest tend to stay at rest. If a person is used to doing nothing to better his or her circumstances, that person is likely to continue to do nothing. If a person is proactive and mindful, that person is likely to continue in that regard.

Underachieving people will not view forces in their lives as mutable. That is to say, such people believe that everything is stagnant. They wil believe that their abilities cannot change, that their performances canno change, that they are either smart or not smart, creative or not creative, hardworking or not hardworking. Their thinking is black and white and full of stigmatic labels.

No matter where you stand, at the bottom in the dark, or at the top feeling bright, you can *always* improve. There are simple and complicated steps that you can take. There are plenty of things you can incorporate into your life. Your daily life.

Let's call them… *Confidence Strategies.*

Powerful Strategies for Success

People can be confident in things and not attempt them. You may be confident that you can make a good low-level manager, but you may never attempt it because you feel you have nothing to prove.

A confident person will attempt things that truly challenge them. But more so, things that *inspire* them.

Still, we have to be realistic. Before you jump into writing the next global best-seller, or set your eyes on being the first to set foot on Saturn, you need to take the small steps to ensure that you're as confident and happy as you can to be.

Try the following list. A lot of it is commonsense, but not commonly applied.

1.   **Smiley Face**—Yes, that's a smile. Not an emoticon, a smile. Research shows that smiling during stressful situations can help lower heart rate levels and jumpstart positive feelings. The physical motion actually makes you more relaxed and pleasant. It triggers neurotransmitters in the brain. It's good for you—do it!

2.   **Kind Acts**—Volunteer somewhere. Send baked goodies, a thank you note, a get-well-soon, wish somebody a happy birthday, hold the door, make somebody dinner—you get the idea. The point is, when you help others you understand that you are powerful and can make a difference in some shape or form. View people as generally good, and seek to further that good. You will feel happier and more confident. Life is too short to spend disliking others. Don't waste time harboring

negative feelings—go out and spread the good.

3. **Take a Compliment**—People with low self-confidence will downplay compliments or ignore them altogether. Some people will even perceive some ulterior motive behind completely harmless compliments.

Stop that! Feel good that somebody cares enough just to say somethin̶ Most people mean it. Whenever you're feeling down, remember the compliments and pull yourself back up.

Guess what? Somebody appreciates you!

4. **Dress Nicely**—This doesn't mean you have to wear an expensive suit or dress. It means wear something that you like, that says, *this is me*. Be something cool. Be spunky, be sophisticated, slick, nerdy, goofy, hippy, comfortable—be you. And love the skin you're in.

5. **Exercise**—Tired of hearing this one? Well it's true! Exercise improves your mood, relieves stress, and over time can completely change your outlook on life. We can talk about specific neural chemicals or weight loss or muscle gain, but the bottom line is pretty simple: it's great for you!

You don't have to be a marathoner or a competitive cross-fitter. Just ̶ in like 20-30 minutes when you can. And don't say that you don't ha̶ time. If you can't carve out 20 minutes just a few times a week, you need to chill out and maybe stop dedicating so much time to other things. Remember, this is your life. *Your* life.

6. **Good Posture**—Sound silly? Well, the studies think otherwise. Slouching comes across negatively and also ruins your posture over time. Stand upright and relax your shoulders. Keep your chin up and your eyes straight. You'll feel more confident, look more confident, and enjoy improved core and better breathing. So stand tall and don't fall.

7. **Good Food**—Another obvious one. Fast food all the time will make you mentally and physically sluggish. A poor diet will lead to health problems and depression. Preparing a nice meal is easier and more enjoyable than most people think. A lot of people claim that they don't have the time or energy, but this is false. Google "quick easy healthy recipes" and enjoy the feast! You might discover a culinary talent you never knew you had.

8. **Friendly Thought**—Tell yourself that most people are good people, and that if you treat them how *you* want to be treated, they will, in return, treat you how *you* want to be treated. Easy enough?

Besides, why would you assume that people dislike you? Are you really that bad? Is everybody else really so focused on *your* perceived faults and failures? You think?

Truth is, most people are too caught up in their own thoughts and insecurities to worry about yours. So be friendly, assume that people are nice, and stop worrying so much. You'll be surprised how kind some people can be when you treat them right.

9. **Organization**—Get your shit straight. I'm not talking about becoming squeaky clean and OCD. I simply suggest that organizing your materials, and your non-materials (thoughts, emotions, feelings), can do amazing things for you.

Organize things in a way that is manageable. Don't get overwhelmed. Find your path and follow it with conviction.

10.**Meditation**—Many people think that meditation is a load of b.s. Meditation promotes stress reduction, relaxation, and productivity. It also helps with depression, blood pressure, and heart disease. Brain strength, measured in the amount of gyrification, or folding of brain tissue, is increased through meditation. So meditate, and see things more clearly!

11.**Me-Time**—Make me-time a priority, especially when you've been going through stressful times. Learn to love yourself instead of berating yourself for occasional missteps. You're human for crying out loud!

Occasionally set aside time for a movie night, or a night out, or some guilty pleasure. Take a long, warm bath. Enjoy a fine liqueur. Remember, part of living life is enjoying pleasure. This doesn't mean we have to go off-the-rocker, but behaving a little 'naughty' from time to time is totally fine.

12.**Mirror Mind**—Break away from the mirror. Unless you're practicing strong eye contact or funny impersonations, you probably shouldn't be spending so much time looking in the mirror. Research shows that frequent 'mirror-gazing' increases insecurities about self-image. It's one thing to want to look good before going out in public. It's another thing to spend so much time getting 'spruced up,' that you never actually get out.

13.**Test Yourself**—That's right, challenge time. Put yourself in a new situation. Say hi to strangers. Enter a competition, go to a concert, read a new book, take up a new hobby. The point is simple: pushing yourself and learning to deal with difficulties. When you push through and persevere, you win. Don't let fear get in the way; prove to yourself how powerful you really are.

Get off the couch and out of your comfort zone!

Life is full of opportunities for people to bloom. We can all take the simple daily steps necessary for boosting our self-images and getting healthier, happier, and stronger. Confidence can enter all areas of our lives. We can all do it.

But sometimes, we need extra help. Sometimes, despite every shred of advice and every garnet of knowledge, we can still falter.

Many times, in order to conquer our lives, we must conquer our feelings. And the only way to conquer our feelings, is to bring them to the surface.

We cannot hide from our feelings. We may think that we can hide from them, because then they can't hurt us.

But they will. They'll bubble up, they'll burst out, they'll bang and bruise our minds and bodies till the end of days. If we try to suppress our feelings, we are only hurting ourselves.

And if we don't face them, we will never fix them…

Control Your Emotions and Stop Floundering!

Dealing with feelings can be tough.

Not just because feelings sometimes seem to strike us at the core, but because they can also lead to a variety of other cognitive and behavioral states. Furthermore, cognitive and behavioral states can lead to a variety of feelings, meaning that it's all thrown into the same, intense cycle.

Strong feelings can make us cry, laugh, yell, scream, and jump up and down, up and down, down and up on our couches like wild people.

Weak feelings may trickle and trickle until they build up and the dam breaks. Whether strong or weak, feelings find their way into our deepest crevices, get under our skin, and can inspire greatness, failure, and everything in between.

But all this talk begs a question, a simple question. What in the world are feelings? Have people actually defined what they are and how they work?

Seriously, think of a feeling. Any feeling—sadness, happiness, contentment, pleasure, pain, envy, sympathy—anything.

Now define it.

Kinda hard, isn't it? You're probably struggling to find the right words to depict what exactly a feeling is, aren't you? Before we talk about working on our feelings, we should probably know what a feeling is..

Researchers have been tackling this very topic for years, and they too have had a great deal of trouble explaining it. In fact, there are so man puzzling and confounding theories and conceptual frameworks out there, that sometimes it seems like we've only gotten *further* from an understanding.

Still, we do have a framework; a scaffolding. The three main concepts to remember are known collectively as *affective phenomena*, meaning that each of them constitutes some sort of emotional expression. How that expression looks depends upon a whole slew of things, and it is n limited to cognitions, preconceptions, sensations and behavioral reactions.

The first affective phenomenon is one you probably haven't heard of. It's called "core affect" and it *affects* you at the core. Get it?

Yea, me neither. Let's look deeper…

Core affect is basically defined by many researchers as a simple, primordial non-reflective feeling common in moods and emotions but always accessible to consciousness. Basically, core affect is the most simple of the three concepts. It is considered "neurophysiological," meaning that we can recognize it in our bodies and our minds. Examples include tension and relaxation, or energy and lethargy. Cor affect can have varying intensities and durations. It is the rawest and most core-based of the three concepts.

The second concept is the idea of emotion. Among researchers of *affective phenomena,* emotion is a multifaceted concept. It is a concept that includes the first concept of "core affect" as well as many others. These many events link together and are directed toward an 'object,' whether that object is a person, place, or thing. That 'object' doesn't even have to be real or present. It can be imagined and from the past or future.

The concept of emotion consists of the following 7 sub-events: (1) core affect, (2) observable behavior alongside the emotion (a frown, a smile, etc.), (3) attention toward the 'object,' (4) cognitive assessment of the meaning and consequences of the 'object' stimulus, (5) attributing the start of the emotion to the 'object,' (6) the experience of the emotion, and (7) neural and endocrine changes correlated with the emotion.

In non-scientific terms, emotions are episodes elicited by something and about something, with the cognitive assessment of person and 'object' constituting the central element. Emotions are a maelstrom of thoughts, feelings, behaviors, and neurophysiological changes. They are certainly a confusing thing…

And to make things more confusing, here is the third and final concept: "mood." In a nutshell, moods usually last longer than emotions. Moods are more global as opposed to specific emotions. Emotions contain reactions to 'objects.' Moods don't really relate to anything in specific.

Take for instance a person who is angry. The emotion is anger and this person is angry at his best friend. In this case, his best friend forgot to pick him up from school.

In another case, a person is in a "shitty mood." When asked why, the person can't really say. Maybe it's because of that annoying woman at the store, or the engine problems with the car, and then not to mention the rent is late, and earlier with the stubbed toe and so now it's blue and he thinks he needs to go the doctor, and then he'll have to…

"Mood" is also not temporally related. You can wake up in the mornin in a bad mood and not know why. Emotions usually follow 'objects' closely in time. Moods typically do not.

OKAY. So now that we've gone over some of the more scholarly and technical aspects of the emotional nature, it's probably time to talk about *coping* with that emotional nature.

Emotions don't have to be necessarily good or bad. Anger can bring somebody to step outside their bounds and fight for what is right. On the flip side, happiness—usually considered 'good'—can lead a person to celebrate excessively, get too drunk, and make foolish decisions.

Using your emotions for positive outcomes is what's most important. That's not to say, you can go and manipulate to make yourself feel better. What it does say is: interpret your feelings, understand them, ar act on them.

If you get irate don't go out and punch somebody or rashly file some ill-conceived lawsuit. Instead, understand why you are angry, ask yourself if it is warranted, and decide how you can make a positive difference using this anger as a driving force.

It's better to understand and act positively on your feelings, even negative feelings, than it is berate yourself for having those feelings.

Some people have the problem of censorship. They suppress all their feelings so much that they become numb. Even when they have the right to show emotion, they feel nothing. Other people, of course, do everything when they have no right to.

Naturally, there are going to be times when you are unable to express what you feel. Identifying your feelings may require you to take a break, a step back, and actually look inward.

You might want to heed your body. Most feelings are experienced in the body. Anxiety might show up as sweaty palms and a raised heart rate. Sadness might show as a weariness of your muscles and sluggishness in your thoughts. All bodies are different, so learn *your* body's responses and don't rely on the experiences of others.

Feelings feed into behaviors. If you don't know what you're feeling, you might try to infer from your behaviors and how other people are reacting. If your voice is shaky and squeaky, you might be nervous. If there is sternness to your tone, you might be angry and not even realize it.

Making the connection between life's events and your feelings is super useful. When you recognize what makes you feel a certain way, you may then more clearly understand and express your feelings to yourself and others.

The problem with feeling a certain way due to events is that it's all subjective. There is no objective standard of a given core affect, emotion, or mood. We aren't responding to events, we're responding to our interpretations and judgments of those events. Our interpretations of events link our feelings to events.

It's that easy. But it's also that bad. See, a lot of times our emotions end up winning. Instead of using our emotions as springboards for personal growth, we get caught up in them. We end up allowing these feelings to penetrate all areas of life, making it even more difficult to feel good.

The bottom line is pretty self-explanatory. Understanding and *utilizing* our feelings makes us feel good. When we feel good, we feel confident. When we feel confident, we feel good.

Still, we must learn to weed out the completely unproductive feelings. Here are some negative tendencies that kill confidence:

- **Black and White Thinking**: We'll see things as good or bad, great or terrible. We'll view our worlds as existing in extremes, when most of what we encounter lies in the murky middle. Emotions can lead us to great inspiration, but they can also destroy us. Sometimes, being levelheaded is the best choice.

- **Egocentrism**: Thinking about ourselves can be good for boosting confidence, but when we constantly attribute negative things to ourselves, the outlook becomes problematic. Just because your friend is in a bad mood, doesn't mean it's because of something you did. You have to be realistic.

- **Generalization**: We all sometimes blow things out of perspective. A minor event is not going to change our life, even if in the moment we think it's "the end." By realizing how much control we have over our lives, we can stop fretting the small stuff.

- **Filtering**: People with low confidence will selectively remember bad events over good times. As a result, these immortal memories *tinge* our overall memories, leading to generalization. We should strive to stop discounting positive events in favor of inflating negative ones. Remember, the emotional effect of an event is dependent largely on the weight we assign to that event.

So stop freaking out!

- **Emotional rationalizing**: Too often we will accept our emotions as immutable fact. If we feel awkward or stupid, we may come to accept these adjectives as inherently part of us. We may actually find ways to demean ourselves.

We need to stop finding ways to hurt ourselves.

Instead, focus on your positive emotions. Let your positive emotions dictate your general state. Next time you feel bad, tell yourself that it's just transient. Next time you feel *good*, tell yourself that it's permanent.

Believing is doing.

Remember again, you *choose* how to cope with your feelings. You choose how to interpret them, how to use them, and even how to express them to family and friends. Sometimes, discretion is the primary goal. Other times, you're best off letting it all out.

To be more confident, we need control. We need to gain control over external and internal processes of our daily lives. We need to interpret feelings in a way that enables adaptive cognitions and behaviors. We want to create a cycle of positivity that reinforces growth in all areas of life.

We're here to bloom, not *wilt*.

Next time your feelings have too much power in your life, take a step back and ask yourself some simple questions:

- Does the intensity of my feelings correspond with the circumstances?

- Do I have more than one feeling that I'm dealing with?

- What are my interpretations?

- In what ways can I express myself?

- What are the effects of these expressions on me?

- What are the effects of these expressions on others?

- What conclusion am I seeking?

- What do I wish to do?

- Would it be better if I did nothing?

Dealing with feelings is a part of dealing with confidence. It can be argued that confidence is only a feeling. It can be argued that confidence is a very real physiological thing.

Truth be told, the nature of confidence and its causes can be explored many ways, by many thinkers. However, what continues to be less debatable are the many positive effects of confidence.

Not having confidence is a terrible thing. Having confidence is a wonderful thing. Everybody wants to feel good. Nobody wants to flounder and sink. Nobody wants to feel like life is too much.

Growing more confident is like blooming. When something blooms, it evolves. It gains a healthy and attractive appearance, it gains vitality, it gains meaning and purpose and isn't afraid to show it.

When people bloom, they learn to soak in the sun and breathe. They learn to focus less on cloudy days and more on the powerful days that lie ahead. They learn to *make* days meaningful by simply believing so.

Soon, our minds create our realities. And our realities, in turn, create us…

Think Fast, Think Smart, Think Before You Start

But what if the world we envision and world we create are two different worlds? What if the gap is glaring? What if it's a *chasm*?

Sometimes, low confidence cannot be treated with self-help alone. Sometimes, we require therapy. When therapeutic intervention is a must, we must be honest with ourselves. Are we willing to listen to a therapist? Or are we simply doing it to appease somebody else?

Goal directed therapy is one of the most prevalent therapies for people with low self-confidence. This form of therapy can be delivered in a variety of ways. It can be administered through a cognitive behavioral approach, through group settings, through brief strategic therapy and even by exposing patients to animals such as cats, dogs, and monkeys.

Group therapy, for one, is very good for those who feel isolated. When you are around other people who express similar struggles, you instantly feel a connection. You begin to realize that life is an amazing process and that everybody else is at different stages in their own process. You also realize that such a process can be redirected.

If things are on the wrong track, hit the brakes and whip the wheel.

Another approach to treating low self-confidence is cognitive behavioral therapy. Cognitive behavioral therapy uses a practical approach in which the therapist fosters a relationship among beliefs, feelings, and thoughts, and their effects on behavioral patterns. The patient learns that his or her perceptions directly affect behaviors and thoughts regarding life circumstances. By changing these things, the individual is able to get to the root of the problem.

CBT employs various approaches in order to create a dynamic technique. Therapists make use of strategies such as journaling, questioning beliefs, open-mindedness, and relaxation. These strategies allow patients to recognize unrealistic perceptions and maladaptive behaviors. Most patients in CBT will continue therapy for many months, typically in hour-long sessions.

If you are willing to undergo therapy, you are recognizing that your lo self-esteem is a significant problem in your life. This is good. It means you're serious about self-improvement, and not just going through the motions.

A lot of people will just go through the motions. They'll do very little here, and very little there, and by the end of the day, every day, they'll be in the same spot.

Feeling lousy and lame.

Confident people never allow feelings like these to last. Confident people do not apologize for having strength that others do not. Confident people do not feel bad about acting when others are afraid to do so. Confident people do not cry or crumble or attack others when things go wrong.

Being confident is not about rolling over people. That is arrogance.

Being confident means that you act when others are too weak to do so. You may encourage. You may reinforce. You may lend a helping hand. You may serve as a moral beacon.

But the bottom line is: *you* are doing it. Not somebody else. Not a friend, not a foe, not some Joe Schmoe off the streets.

By reducing self-consciousness, confidence allows us to endure a variety of effects. Tough feelings, social pressures, disparaging remarks, and stern judgments can all be handled readily and impersonally.

We learn not to lose ourselves in self-evaluation.

Confidence boosts awareness and gives us power. Instead of reacting automatically in a negative way, we react thoughtfully in a positive one. Instead of responding bitterly, retreating in fear, or thoughtlessly indulging an impulse, we get the opportunity to speak to ourselves.

They say that knowledge is power. But without confidence, what will you do with that knowledge? Where will you derive that power?

If somebody tries to take your power, you take it right back. When you're right and *they* are wrong, there is no reason to feel bad. If you rise to the top while others sink low, there is no reason to feel bad. If your weaknesses are stronger than another person's greatest strengths, there is no reason to feel bad. If you simply go after things while others are afraid, there is *certainly* no reason to feel bad.

If you seize success while others fumble in failure, *that* is confidence.

No apologies accepted.

You might be in a room with a bunch of people, and know nothing of anyone.

But that doesn't stop you from feeling fine about who you are.

You might be surrounded by beautiful women at a bar. You might be surrounded by amazing guys at a pub. Whatever your sexual preference, you stay your ground and keep your cool.

You let them know you got it. And when you got it, you *got* it.

Got it?

Staying confident should never interfere or conflict with something else. Confidence is an increase not a decrease. Being confident should improve relationships. Having confidence *improves* social status and career position. Remaining confident *improves* sex drive and physical shape.

One's confidence should never conflict with one's duties. We do what we have to do because we're confident. We're confident that we'll take it somewhere. We're confident that we can make it happen.

Perhaps you are insecure or unhappy. It could be that you lack direction, that time after time after time you believe you've wasted your time. Maybe it's that you struggle because you don't know any other way—you have failed to diversify, to go out into the world and discover other people, places, and things.

In every walk of life there are people who will try to bring you down. These are the same people who tell you that you are not good enough, that you're not smart enough, pretty enough, strong enough, hard-working enough. These people will ignore their own issues and problems in order to find fault in yours.

But these people don't matter. Because the only voice that matters is the voice that comes from within.

And this begins with loving ourselves for everything that we've done. For everything that we haven't done.

So tell yourself this. Tell it to yourself every day.

And watch. Every day, every moment, you'll feel a little less regretful, a little less critical of your 'failures.'

Treating low self-confidence must begin with the origin of the problem. If we feel that we can't possibly pull ourselves up, we need to rethink our stance. Are there others who can help us? Are we willing to admit that we need help?

After all, even if we acknowledge that others can help us, we are not saved. It is ultimately up to the individual with the problem to defeat it. At times when the support network is missing, then what? Will we slip back into self-pity, or will we cultivate the power to care for ourselves.

Firstly, don't expect to beat it easily. Low self-confidence can always return. Boosting self-esteem is about changing the way we think about *everything*. It is literally an overhaul of our life perspective.

Beating self-esteem is about finding an informed psychiatrist, and not some family doctor who may know us, but not therapeutic methods. It about understanding that the loss of a life and the change of a life do not have to bring us down. It is about staring unflinchingly into the eye of utter blackness and *choosing* sight over suffering.

It is about meeting new people and having new beliefs and finding new ways to navigate this slippery slope we sometimes call life. Finding happiness is about taking time to change, allowing time to start anew; grow, to fumble, to fail, to find, somewhere in the struggle, something *worth* the struggle.

There is no telling how many chances we get in this fragile thing called life, but there is always reason to change. Boosting low self-esteem may be the hardest thing in the world to do. We are fighting our brains. We are fighting our environment. We are fighting the very thing that forms our being.

But we are not alone. And believe me you, there is a beautiful world out there just waiting…

And if we want it bad enough, we can get it.

So tomorrow morning when you wake up, stop feeling bad for yourself. Look in the mirror, for a bit, and tell yourself what you've never said or believed. Realize that just because you are not 'the best' at this or that, you are still going to do the best *you* can do.

Believe it, feel it, and do it. Stop shriveling away, and stop making excuses. It's time to look into the sun—you owe it to yourself.

Bloom.

About The Author

C.K. Murray is a world traveler, inquisitor, and hobbyist. He's worked in various careers from education to geriatrics, and enjoys spending free time with his girlfriend, and best friend, in the Pacific Northwest.

Born in 1959, Murray lived a whimsical childhood. It wasn't until his teenage years that life became a little less rosy. In the 70s, Murray endured several family mishaps and an unfortunate skiing accident. He began experimenting with drugs soon thereafter, and learned firsthand the pains and horrors of addiction. Following a brief period of recovery Murray again slipped into addiction.

For years, Murray was in and out of treatment programs. He landed in outpatient and inpatient recovery, weekend interventions, 28-day rehabilitations, and a variety of transitional housing for addiction.

Still, nothing seemed to be working.

In order to support his habits, Murray resorted to petty theft and constant manipulation. He exploited close friends and family, confidantes and acquaintances—anybody who had not given up on him He betrayed the people who loved him the most, all in the name of chasing that next, great 'high.'

But then something struck. After watching fellow addicts wither and die, Murray began to realize what he had spent his entire life denying: that nobody was going to save him.

After a long bout with depression and the criminal justice system in the 90s, Murray finally kicked the habit. He is currently in his 8th year of sobriety and continues to this day to attend addiction and rehabilitation meetings. He is a member of Narcotics Anonymous (NA) and Alcoholics Anonymous (AA), and a firm believer in the 12-step program.

His efforts as a motivational speaker and counselor have helped numerous addicts to rediscover meaning in their lives.

Other works by C.K. Murray:

1. _Mindfulness Explained: The Mindful Solution to Stress, Depression, and Chronic Unhappiness_

2. _Emotional Intelligence Explained: How to Master Emotional Intelligence and Unlock Your True Ability_

3. _The Confidence Cure: Your Definitive Guide to Overcoming Low Self-Esteem, Learning Self-Love and Living Happily_

4. _Let Love Flourish: The Secret to Finding Your Kindred Heart_

5. *Body Language Explained: How to Master the Power of the Unconscious*

6. *Hair Loss Explained: Natural Solutions for Hair Loss and Premature Balding*

7. *The Omega Factor: 20 SUPERCHARGED Omega-3 Recipes for the Body and Mind*

8. *A Reason to Smile: Finding Happiness in Life's Little Moments*

9. *Health Hacks: 46 Hacks to Improve Your Mood, Boost Your Performance, and Guarantee a Longer, Healthier, More Vibrant Life*

10. *Depression, Drugs, & the Bottomless Pit: How I found my light amid the dark*

11.   *The Stress Fallacy: Why Everything You Know Is WRONG*

12.   *Master Mind: Unleashing the Infinite Power of the Latent Brain*

13.   *Sex Science: 21 SIZZLING Secrets That Will Transform Your Bedroom into a Sauna*

14.   *Sex Secrets: How to Conquer the Power of Sexual Attraction*

15.   *Master of the Game: A Modern Male's Guide to Sexual Conquest*

16.   *Persuasion Explained: How to Use Your Inner Eye to Influence Others*

17.   *Deep Sleep: 32 Proven Tips for Deeper, Longer More Rejuvenating Sleep*

18.   *Win Back Your Ex! The Secrets to Rekindling Your Relationship*

19.   *The Blood Pressure Diet: 30 Recipes Proven fo Lowering Blood Pressure, Losing Weight, and Controlling Hypertension*

20.   *Coconut Oil Cooking: 30 Delicious and Easy Coconut Oil Recipes Proven to Increase Weight Loss and Improve Overall Health*

21.   *High Blood Pressure Explained: Natural, Effective, Drug-Free Treatment for the "Silent Killer"*

22. *The Wonders of Water: How H2O Can Transform Your Life*

23. *INFUSION: 30 Delicious and Easy Fruit Infused Water Recipes for Weight Loss, Detox, and Vitality*

24. *The Ultimate Juice Cleanse: 25 Select Juicing Recipes to Optimize Weight Loss, Detox and Longevity*

25. *ADHD Explained: Natural, Effective, Drug-Free Treatment For Your Child*

26. *How to Help an Alcoholic: Coping with Alcoholism and Substance Abuse*

27.   *Vitamin D Explained: The Incredible, Healing Powers of Sunlight*

28.   *Last Call: Understanding and Treating the Alcoholic Brain (A Personal and Practical Guide)*

29.   *Hooked: Life Lessons of an Alcoholic and Addic (How to Beat it Before it Beats YOU)*

30.   *Fragmented: Piecing Together the Mind of an Addict*

31.   *Neuro-Linguistic Programming Explained: You Definitive Guide to NLP Mastery*

32.   *Hooking Up: A College Guy's Guide to Wild Fu*

Casual Sex, and Campus Companionship

33.   *Natural Weight Loss: PROVEN Strategies for Healthy Weight Loss & Accelerated Metabolism*

34.   *BEAT The Hangover: Your Ultimate Guide to Drinking, Partying and Waking up Hangover Free*

Printed in Great
Britain
by Amazon